LIVING SINGLE

FORTY AND BEYOND

LIVING SINGLE

COPYRIGHT © 2016 BY Cindy Surniak. ALL RIGHTS RESERVED.

No part of this publication may be reproduced, stored in a retrieval system or transmitted in any way by any means, electronic, mechanical, photocopy, recording or otherwise without the permission of the author except as provided by the USA copyright law.

Scripture quotations have been taken from the Holy Bible, New International Version Copyright 1996, used by permission by Zondervan Corporation. All rights reserved.

Written by Cindy Surniak
Cover design and photography by Cindy Surniak
Editor in Chief Sandra A. LaSalle
Assistant Editor Cynthia I. Nakaya

About the Author

Cindy has worked as a nurse for twenty-seven years, also using her skills on short-term mission trips in the US and abroad, and in caring for several foster children in her home. She knows the pain of loss, physical illness, clinical depression and the pain and joys that accompany the single life. She has written two books, Where Are You, God? and a children's book, Noah and The Ark. Her recent hobbies are painting, writing, photography and travel. She now works and resides in Florida.

Table of Contents

1. Our Heart's Desire
2. Sometimes God Says, "No!"
3. Gods Protection
4. Sexual Purity
5. Yes, I'm Alone!
6. Adam and Eve
7. Why Are You Single?
8. A Grumbling Spirit
9. A Cross to Bear
10. Fitting In
11. You Will Survive

Introduction

I sat there listening…listening to yet another happily married man teach on how to live a happy single life. Most of these men have several children and many grandchildren to sit on their laps. From the sound of their testimonies, I doubt they have ever been alone for more than a few days at a time.

After listening for many years, I personally felt these men and their wives were not qualified to teach on the single life since many of these couples married soon after high school or college. I often prayed God would send older qualified singles to teach on this subject. After all, they would know better than anyone what it is like to live single.

This book is about my story. It speaks to the older single. It spans over twenty years of dating, desiring and praying for God's man to "sweep me off my feet." I want every single person who reads this book to know that I understand your pain and loneliness. My prayer is that you will wait for God's best, no matter what that may be.

~Cindy

1

Our Heart's Desire

Delight in the Lord, and He will give you the desires of your heart.
Psalm 37:4

If I heard it once, I heard it countless times from married friends and family who meant well, "Cindy, God gives you the desires of your heart." What my friends didn't tell me about this verse when I was young in the Lord and what I failed to understand all those years was this: I needed to first 'delight' in the Lord.

The word delight in Hebrew means: To be pliable and soft. This word "delight" tells me I need to have a soft, pliable spirit towards God and His will.

I look back and admit most of my time was spent grumbling about my single life instead of delighting in the Lord. I was taught from the first day I was saved not to base anything on feelings. Feelings are fickle. Base everything on the Word of God.

Unfortunately, my feelings ruled on this subject. I wanted to fall in love, get married, have ten children, a few dogs and live happily ever after. Despite all the blessings God gave me I focused on one thing—marriage. I couldn't understand why all my friends were marrying and my desire was being ignored. I felt unloved, useless, and incomplete. I struggled with sermons that taught the single life is a blessing and a gift from God. I reasoned, *"If this is such a great gift, why don't many people want it?"* Most singles want to marry and have a family and they usually follow this path. At the same time, I struggled with singles who said they were content and I wondered why I didn't feel the same way. My desire was to be content, because in Philippines 4:11 God's desire for me is to be content in all things. The guilt consumed me at times—"What is wrong with me?" I often pondered. The more I dwelt on seeking contentment and the more time passed, the more withdrawn I became to the point I no longer cared. My struggle with God's promise of contentment now entered into a state of hopelessness. My friend, that is dangerous territory!

After many years of struggling with Psalms 37:4, I discovered I need to first delight in God no matter what my desire may be. I learned I need to enjoy His presence and take great pleasure sitting at His feet even if no one was beside me. When we delight in God, we have no time to grumble about those things to which God says, "No!" Our heart's desire will match God's desire. This may be singleness for some.

2

Sometimes God Says, "No!"

The year 2012 was not a great year for me. It seemed with every turn I was either sick, having surgery or stressed by the lack of money to pay my monthly bills. The mental, physical, and financial pain never seemed to stop. To make a bad situation worse, I was totally alone; I had no one to help me out of my mess. I prayed daily, "Please help me, Lord!"

I remember, it was June and I woke up to a warm summer breeze coming through my window. Today was the day...a day I never wanted. I would have THE surgery. I fought against it for almost ten years. I knew in my heart that God would fulfill His promise to me. He would still give me the desire of my heart.
I reasoned I would be like Sarah: giving birth beyond my reproductive years.

But that hope was slowly fading away. With an intense burning in my abdomen and lower back, I was doubled over in pain most days and unable to function. I finally relented and had a consultation with my doctor. I pleaded with her to be conservative as she considered surgery. I did not want to lose my ovaries and uterus all at once, not yet. Hormones have a great impact on a woman, physically and mentally. I was afraid of crashing and slipping into a depression. But there was another reason, a secret one. In the deepest part of my soul, I knew one day I would have a baby. I just knew I would be a Sarah. I reasoned that God would give me triplets fulfilling my desire of a family with one pregnancy. I even named these future children. How silly, right?

My doctor indeed was conservative and the surgery was a success. The football size fibroid was removed along with the lining of my uterus. Now no baby would be able to attach and grow there. The ablation procedure damaged my uterine lining which is needed to bring a baby to term. In my heart I knew that was not a problem. I still had my uterus and ovaries. I knew God was able to repair my lining and all would be well.

Six months later, it was time for my follow-up appointment with my doctor to assess the results of the surgery via ultrasound. It revealed my uterus was back to normal size, but my ovaries told a different story. They looked abnormal and this time a total hysterectomy was advised.

Stunned, I walked out of her office holding back tears. Psalms 37:4 now seemed like a cruel joke to me. How would I see the fulfillment of this desire, a good desire to have a child? My long awaited dream now turned into hopelessness. During the past thirty years of walking with the Lord I never questioned the sound doctrine I learned about God, until I received this news. "When will I see my heart's desire of having my own children and why was God saying no?!"

Within two weeks, I was lying on the operating table. Many friends offered to be with me at the hospital yet I refused. By this time, my heart was cut in two and I felt if God wanted me alone in life, so be it…I would be alone. I had one friend drive me to the hospital and afterwards drive me home after the surgery.

The surgery went well. I remember the staff lifting me off the table and placing me in a reclining chair. I was groggy and could not seem to awaken. I recall hearing the nurse tell someone to have my friend come to take me home. I remember thinking I was not in any condition to leave.

"Cindy, Cindy wake up!" My friend was now sitting next to me.

Within a short time, they transferred me to a wheelchair. I felt nauseous so they gave me a basin to hold… just in case. Moments later, they escorted me to the car with the basin under my chin. What's wrong with this picture? As a nurse, I complained to the doctor about my minimal time of recuperation. It was clear they wanted me out of their hospital no matter what my condition may be.

I remember praying in the car, "God, just get me home before I get sick." He did. I told my friend I would be fine and she left. I did not realize there would be a problem walking up a flight of stairs. I did not realize a little incision would be so painful. I could not climb the stairs and no one was there to help. On all fours, I crawled up one step at a time. I made it to my bedroom but I was unable to lift myself to the bed. I laid there for a few minutes, then slowly got to my knees and then my feet. Sitting on the edge of the bed, I slowly laid down and fell asleep. I slept for quite a while, was it an hour, three hours or a day? I awoke to dozens of messages on my phone from concerned family and friends. They truly sought to hear of my condition and if there was a way they could help. In my heart I was thrilled I had family and friends who cared and loved me, yet I was struggling emotionally as my 'desire' was just ripped away from me. The promise God gave in Psalms 37:4 to give me the desires of my heart no longer applied to me. With tears in my eyes, I questioned, "WHY?"

I am grateful for my surgeon. We both agreed to be conservative. In surgery, she saw only one ovary needed to be removed. I was grateful because I worried if I had a total hysterectomy my hormones would plummet and send me into a depression. She observed my left ovary was completely destroyed and my right was impaired yet functional.

The healing process was brutal. I could not cough, sneeze, or leave my bed without excruciating pain. I seriously could not believe cutting a half inch incision in my abdomen would cause this much pain. It was during the second week of healing I started to mend and refocus. I questioned, "Why God did You say NO to the desire of my heart?!"

Prior to my surgery I was reading through the Chronological Bible along with my audio Bible app. Every time I got to the book of Deuteronomy, something would interrupt me. I would doze off to sleep or the phone would ring, which prevented me from completing this book. With resolve, I was determined to read through it without interruption. I never thought God's answer to me would come through the life of Moses (never mind the book of Deuteronomy!).

Below is a quick history regarding Moses leading the Israelites and a passage which pierced my heart. It truly was an answer God longed to share with me. He shared it in His time, waiting for the time when I was unable to move yet able to listen without interruption.

Most of us are familiar with Moses and the burning bush, the parting of the Red Sea and his time on the mountain receiving the Ten Commandments from God to give to His people. Moses was considered a friend of God: a close friend. He was also a prophet. He was chosen by God to lead several million people to the Promised Land—the land over the Jordan filled with riches and plenty of food and water. Yet the Israelites sinned and rebelled. A thirteen day journey ended up taking forty years of wandering in the desert. Moses led people who were obstinate complainers and had to deal with them on a daily basis. Could you imagine dealing with several million people who were never happy or satisfied? Moses handled these complainers and did a great job. I reasoned, if I were Moses and served God so faithfully through difficulties, I would think God would reward me with the desire of my heart, right? In Moses' case, his desire was to enter into Jordan, yet God said no.

Moses shared with the people he led. In Deuteronomy 3:23-27, Moses said:

> At that time, I pleaded with the Lord: "O' Sovereign Lord, you have begun to show to Your servant Your greatness and strong hand. For what god is there in heaven or on earth who can do the deeds and mighty works You do? Let me go over and see the good land beyond the Jordan—that fine hill country and Lebanon." But because of you the Lord was angry with me and would not listen to me. "That is enough!" the Lord said. "Do not speak to me anymore about this matter. Go up to the top of Pisgah and look west and north and south and east. Look at the land with your own eyes, since you are not going to cross this Jordan."

First, did you notice how Moses pleaded for the Lord to give him the desire of his heart? He pleaded. He did not just ask, but pleaded. After wandering in the desert for forty years, leading an obstinate people, God said "no" to Moses' heart's desire. The reason—he struck a rock to bring forth water, when God told him only to speak to it (Numbers 20:11-12). God took his heart's desire and said "No!" In fact, God said, "Enough! Do not speak to me anymore about this matter."

Was God too harsh with Moses? After all, he only hit a rock. In Numbers 20:12; after Moses hit the rock, God said, "Because you did not trust in me enough to honor me as holy in the sight of the Israelites, you will not bring this community into the land I give them."

It pierced my heart when God said to Moses, "Enough! do not speak to me anymore about this matter." From that point on I stopped speaking to God about bearing a child. He made it clear as I lay on the operating table the answer to me is "No." To my surprise, instead of tears I felt an overwhelming peace. For me, the matter was settled, because I trust God with every aspect of my life. His no was all I needed to hear.

3

God's Protection

The best of friends tried and failed. Many friends who planned to fix me up with my future husband never did. Most of the time divine intervention prevailed. The stories are endless so I will just share a few.

It was late at night when the phone rang. A good friend from three states away had called to let me know she met a wonderful single guy, who would be perfect for me. She described her dinner plans for us to meet. I agreed and boarded a train for a relaxing and fun weekend away. The guy never showed. He called to say he had the flu. He was not trying to back out since he did not know she was playing matchmaker. As I traveled home on the train, I could not, no, did not want to believe God said "no." Again. I traveled all that way for nothing. At that moment, I vowed I would never go anywhere to meet a man. He would come to me.

Another time, a friend who lived an hour away called and invited me to a party being held that night. She confessed she wanted me to meet a friend; a nice guy she thought would be perfect for me. I told her I no longer travel to meet a potential date. If the guy is interested, he needs to come meet me or at least pick up the phone and initiate a call. You may think this is harsh, but like the above story, every time someone wanted to fix me up or the guy wanted to meet me, they would suggest I come to him. I guess I'm old fashioned, but I believe the man should come and pick me up or I would meet him at a public place near my home for safety reasons. When I explained this to my friend she stated, "You are being stubborn and old-fashioned!" In my heart I knew not to go. God made it clear this is not His plan for me, but I reluctantly agreed to go anyway.

Keep in mind it was winter. While I was speaking with her on the phone, there was not a cloud in the sky. An hour later as I opened the door to leave, there was a blizzard in progress. Snow everywhere. I could not possibly risk traveling at night in this snow storm. My mom was shocked when she looked out the window. The forecast did not call for any snow. I never went. I did not know at the time, but I now know that it was divine intervention. God did not want me there. I should have listened to His still small voice. But as you know girls, we single women get a bit bored and do things we ordinarily would not do.

Another friend had a great guy for me to meet. The day my friend invited him to a party to introduce me, he announced he was engaged! He never knew of the plan to meet me.

By this time I was in my mid-thirties and a plan to fix me up again took place without my knowledge. Two friends wanted to play matchmaker. Again to meet "a really nice guy." They all knew by now my 'fix up' history, so they did it privately. I went to a fun party, had lots of laughs and went home. Months later my friends told me they had asked a guy to come to that party. He lived out of state yet said yes. On the way his car broke down and he never made it. Again, neither he nor I knew about the matchmaking plans.

I thank God I never met any of these men. Could you imagine all those rejections!?

For years I could not understand why God always said no to these dates. It's just a date...a free dinner. What's wrong with meeting different men and enjoying their company? He graciously reminded me of a prayer shortly after I got saved. I was eighteen years old. I was young but not stupid. In my parent's home in my bedroom was a little storage space where I would crawl into for some quiet-time. This private space was my prayer closet. I loved it there. It was so peaceful and quiet. I remember my prayer like it was yesterday.

"Lord, if you see divorce, adultery or a drinker in my future, please keep me single."

I knew I would not be able to handle these three issues. I knew what I was praying, but I also knew God is a God of miracles. Not every man divorces his wife or commits adultery with another woman. Not every man drinks or is sarcastic and mean-spirited. There are many nice guys out there. To be honest—I met many suitable men, but I knew in my heart they were not right for me. I can honestly say I have never been in love and I know I never passed up the right guy.

To those few I dated, God said no. And when God takes a man away from you, trust me—let him go.

Father knows best!

4

Sexual Purity

Being sexually faithful is tough. Our old sinful nature is constantly battling with our new nature. Unfortunately, sexual sin seems to be common in the church today. This breaks my heart and I'm sure it breaks the heart of God.

The Bible makes this subject clear, sex outside of marriage is a sin—no exceptions. Sex is for marriage only. When we stray, we are inviting God's judgment right into our bedrooms. God takes sex and the proper use of it seriously. He knows improper use will cause pain and heartache and wishes to spare us from this pain. He is a loving God who wants to protect us from the consequences of sexual sin. There are countless verses and stories that teach sexual purity pleases God. Hebrews 13:4 is a common verse that speaks about keeping the marriage bed pure. King David, Solomon and the church in Corinth along with many other examples in scripture give us one message from God. Stay pure!

When we decide to engage in sexual sin, our relationship with Christ suffers. Those few moments of pleasure hurts our relationship with Him. Does God forgive? Yes, He does, He loves us. His forgiveness is there for us. We need to seek His face, turn from our sin and allow God to heal our wounds.

It's easy to fall into the trap of sexual temptation, none of us are immune to it. Any of us can fall. We all need to get tough in order to avoid it. *When it comes to sexual sin, slap it across the face and never apologize for doing so and then run from it.*

Remember, God's desire should be your desire and it is NEVER God's desire for you to have sex outside of marriage. If you have strayed in this area please know God loves and adores you. He wants to stay in fellowship with you. Repent and cling to your Savior. He is waiting for you with open arms.

Let me leave you with this: When I was sixteen years old I started dating a boy. One morning my dad was driving me to school and asked, "Would you give this boyfriend a million dollars?" I responded with a firm, "no." My dad replied, "Then you don't give him your *purity* because that is worth more."

That was the greatest advice my dad ever gave me. In fact, today girls, I would say *your purity* is priceless.

5

Yes, I'm Alone!

Another Friday night sitting home alone. At this point in time I was on the west coast. I worked evenings, and I was far away from family and friends. I had no close friends around me and most nights were filled with silence. Money was tight. Gone were the trips to Alaska, Bahamas and Mexico. Gone were the days I could just board a plane to fly somewhere—anywhere. I was now living in Southern California. Living there was draining my bank account, my joy and there seemed to be no way out.

By this time in my life I accomplished most of what I wanted. College was behind me, I served the Lord as a foster parent, served in my local church, went on a few mission trips in the US and abroad, and traveled for fun. I moved several times, living in four different states. I bought three homes in six years, while my friends were now married with families of their own. At forty years old, I suddenly realized I was all alone.

As I look back, I realize I concentrated on things I did not have instead of what I did possess. I wasted so much time grumbling over being single when God was piling up blessing after blessing. The hard reality: I would have given up those blessings for a wonderful man, a few kids and the perfect house with the white picket fence. All I ever wanted was to be a stay-at-home mom with a kind-hearted Christian man who loved the Lord and our children. Was that too much to ask?

Now that I'm older, I think one of the worst feelings one can have is loneliness. Once loneliness comes in your life—another enemy walks in: hopelessness.

Hopelessness devastates the soul, but it also brings us to our knees, seeking Christ.

For me, being alone has been filled with tears and a hopelessness no one and nothing could fill, except God. My times of loneliness living out west were filled with sweet fellowship with Jesus. Our late night talks were filled with many tears. But His love, patience and sweet spirit permeated my mind, heart and soul. His presence was so near I did not want the morning to come. When the first rays of sun poked through the sky, I longed for the night to come again so He and I could chat some more. Jesus was always on my mind and I wanted nothing more than to abide in Him every moment of the day. I would listen to his Word as I drifted off to sleep and as I awoke in the morning. His Word comforted my hopeless spirit and calmed my anxious heart. He gave me strength when I had none. And when fear gripped my soul He would whisper from his Word, "Fear not!"

During those days I eagerly studied His Word but it seemed I was running out of answers. The more I dug, the deeper the questions. Again, no one was there to help me. I sought help. Unfortunately, they could not care less that I was drowning in a sea of loneliness, despair and hopelessness. So I turned again to God's Word and I found something I never knew before. The depth of God's love for me was deeper than I imagined; so deep it had no end. I always knew God loved me but now it was different. The knowledge was not enough, I had to experience it. I found His love is deeper and richer than any man's love could ever be.

Am I alone? Yes, I am. But that loneliness has produced a richness and depth in my relationship with God that is unexplainable and I would not want anyone to fill it but Him.

If you are alone, take time to get to know the Man who will never leave nor forsake you. Get to know the depth and richness of His love. When you do, you will never regret those lonely nights again. Instead, you will welcome them.

6

Adam and Eve
Not Sally the single and Bob the bachelor

Throughout the years I was often told the single life is a gift. It surely did not feel like it on those "I feel sorry for myself" days.

My questions were endless: What is wrong with me? Am I too ugly? Am I too fat? Am I too skinny? What am I doing wrong? "Being lonely is extremely painful, Lord. Obeying You sexually is pure torture! Why me? I hate this, God!" To make my misery worse, I had to watch many couples: living, **"happily ever after."**

Being alone, I had a lot of time to ponder these questions, these valid feelings and seek biblical answers. The answers are found right in the beginning, in the Garden.

In Genesis 2:15-25, God explains how He made man and put him in the Garden to care for it. He said there was no suitable helper for Adam. God caused him to go into a deep sleep and created a woman from his rib, Eve. God said in Genesis 2:18, "It is not good for man to be alone, I will make a suitable helper for him."

God makes it clear He made man and woman to help one another. They are designed to leave father and mother and cling to one another for life. There is no mention of God creating Adam and Eve along with "Sally the single" or "Bob the bachelor." **God clearly states being alone is not a good thing** in Genesis 2:18. So why are there so many singles today? Why does God allow it?

There is no mention of singleness in this Genesis passage. God's perfect plan for relationships was for each man to have a wife, marry and have children. Evil destroyed that plan. Adam and Eve disregarded God's plan and listened to Satan. As a result, sin entered the world. Previously, it seemed like marriage was the ideal option for mankind.

There was not a 'single' word spoken about living single before the fall of man.

God, through the apostle Paul, calls the single life a gift and writes about it in First Corinthians chapter seven. For years I could not wait until I went to Heaven to have a long chat about this 'gift': one that I thought was not a gift at all! Like I said in chapter one, "if the single life is such a great gift why don't many people want it?" The advertisements for dating sites alone tell me many are not happy without that significant other to share their lives with. But after many years of learning and growing in faith I now see my error. For some, singleness IS a gift.

When Adam and Eve disobeyed God, everything on the earth was tainted by sin, including relationships. Even though God said it is not good for man to be alone––sometimes it is good to be alone to be spared from the sinful behavior of another. So it is a gift—a great gift.

Adultery, physical, emotional, and sexual abuse, drunkenness coupled with abandonment by a spouse are becoming too familiar within the church. Fortunately, singles never have to deal with these particular issues within a marriage.

When God makes it clear to you the single life is a gift, your calling, there is complete peace. There is no inner conflict. You are at peace with God's decision. Yet for most singles, an intense struggle ensues. Most singles want a significant other and all that comes with the package. Men and women are designed to be dependent on one another; to understand, encourage and help one another through difficult times. We were never meant to live independently from one another, unless one receives a special calling to singleness like the apostle Paul.

7

Why Are You Single?

"Why are you single, Cindy?"
"The men must be blind."
"Of all the woman I know, I do not understand why God would keep you single."
"I cannot imagine you being single for much longer."
"You would be a great mother. Such a shame!"

My mom was old fashion who wanted me to find a man so he could protect and provide for me. She also knew I would make a wonderful wife and mother and have much to offer a man. She could not understand why I was single. Her desire was for me to marry. Once she said in a joking but serious manner, "Your husband must be dead, why else would you be single?"

These are common phrases I heard for years from well-meaning people in and outside the church. Without knowing, they believe that if one is single there is something 'not right' with that individual. These comments discouraged me. I was made to feel incomplete if I did not have a man.

I know I don't have the gift of singleness. I also know God has protected me from marrying the wrong man. Perhaps God said "no" to my desire for the same reason He did with Moses who didn't TRUST God and regard Him as HOLY. In the following two chapters I will share two more reasons why God may be keeping me and you single.

I do know this—after all the failed attempts of friends to bring me a suitable match, and the men I did date—I never once said, 'that's the one.' I never said nor felt I was in love. I can say with complete confidence I never passed up the right guy.

8

A Grumbling Spirit

A few years back I wondered why I never found the right man to marry. I tried my best to be obedient while at the same time I saw girls walk away from God and engage in sexual sin only to find out they were blessed in the end and married a good man. I often argued with God, "Really, Lord? She sins and You give her a good husband, but pass me by?" I feel God does not ignore me nor my desires. Yet it is hard to stay focused and live in obedience when I see their happy lives, shared with a man.

I failed to see the problem with my reasoning. I know I am not better than these women, and my thoughts about them were wrong, but I also thought obedience brought blessings. Yes, in many cases throughout scripture it does, but it also teaches we do not deserve anything from God! His gifts are not given as a reward for our 'goodness' but given freely according to His will and His abundant love so that He might be glorified. This truth is still hard for me to understand. It seems reasonable that God would bless obedience over disobedience every time.

I also learned how my grumbling spirit displeased God. I too became like an Israelite. Throughout their journey with Moses, despite all the blessings from God, they grumbled and complained. He made sure their shoes and clothing never wore thin during those forty years. Yet instead of focusing on God's gifts, they focused on what God did not bestow.

I look back and cringe as I reflect on all my grumblings before God. He was pouring out on me blessings upon blessings, yet instead of having a thankful heart, I grumbled about what He kept from me—a husband and children.

Today, I no longer grumble for what I lack, instead I praise God for giving me all I need through Christ Jesus. Even if He never gives me a husband, my relationship with Him is enough.

9

A Cross To Bear

My spiritual mom, who has known me for 30 years, once said, "Cindy, you desire marriage and children so intensely, perhaps the single life is the cross you must bear." I never thought of singleness as a cross to bear, but after years of careful consideration, I realize she may be right.

God may not grant our desire to marry for several reasons. It could be His protection or our disobedience. There may be a another reason God calls us to a single life. It may be the cross He wants us to carry. When our greatest desire is to obey God; He asks for a life of total submission. Our devotion is to Him and it may be to Him alone. Instead of viewing the single life as a calling, it may be a cross to bear, a hard road He has called us to walk. If marriage and children are a constant desire, a want…feeling like a need in your soul, perhaps the single life is a cross God wants you to endure.

How much are you willing to sacrifice for God? Will you die to self and follow Christ if He keeps the desire of your heart from you? Or out of desperation, will you find someone and marry anyway? Sounds impossible, right? You would never marry if God said no… or would you? Think about it. A good looking, kind hearted man sweeps you off your feet. To your surprise God begins to say no to this wonderful man. What will you do? Will you put your desires aside and put God first or will you marry this man God is clearly saying no to? I think we can all agree breaking up with someone we love is heart-wrenching. God will not force you to break up with him. He will send you warning signs NOT TO MARRY. Will you listen? I am grateful I listened to God. The consequences if I married could have been disastrous.

God may be giving you warning signs to end your dating relationship. Take a quiet moment and truly listen to His still, small voice. The results of biting into that forbidden piece of candy, as sweet as it tastes now, may end in disaster.

10

Fitting In

At my age, being single, never married and without children can be challenging. I simply do not fit in anywhere. I am too old to be part of a college and career group while too young to be playing bingo with the senior citizens. While too single to be hanging out with the married couples, I do not fit in with the divorcees or the singles with children.

Where do I belong? Where do I go and what do I do?

To be honest, I don't know.

It hurts to stick out. It feels uncomfortable to sit alone in church and watch families laugh and enjoy one another. Spending time with friends helps the loneliness but it will never fully satisfy a heart that longs for a husband and family.

I appreciate churches who reach out and offer support groups for all singles. Let's be honest though, who wants to attend a singles group until they die of old age? Unlike marrieds who seem to move on with life, we singles never seem to move beyond the singles group. We are stuck in this single time capsule we can't seem to get out of.

Let me explain: Everyone graduates and moves on. From the time we are born until the day we graduate from high school we are all on the same playing field, but that's where it stops. When school is finished most will seek a career, marry, have children, grandchildren, then great grandchildren. With every life event there is excitement and joy, whether it's their wedding day or watching their five year old graduate from kindergarten. It is not this way for the single person. Life seems to stand still. Singles will never enjoy their wedding day, (the birth of a child, the joy of seeing that child grow in the Lord, get married and give them grandchildren) with a husband by their side. Don't get me wrong, singles have many choices and freedom to do many great things, but at times it would be nice to have that special someone to enjoy them with.

So where do I fit in? Only one place, the Kingdom of God.

Take heart if you do not feel you belong anywhere, because you fit perfectly in the palm of God's hand and His Kingdom. When you allow Jesus to be your main focus in life, He will comfort you in the midst of not fitting in.

11

You Will Survive

The single life brings many challenges. Many of these must be faced alone.

For one, the financial burden can be a huge challenge when there is no one else to help pay the bills. There is no one to tell us how pretty we are, which every woman likes to hear from a man. Alone, we have no one to share our day. The nights too can be dreadful. Every night it's dinner for one. Those lonely nights in bed drag on and no one is there to hug us when we are hurting. Sunday morning the seat next to us remains empty. We serve the Lord alone, do yard work and fix broken appliances alone, buy a house and pay the mortgage alone, buy a car alone, watch television, bike, hike and go on vacations alone. Basically, we do everything alone. We lack that help-mate and companion. The greatest struggle for most singles are the nights when that sexual need is not met. How does it feel knowing you may never be sexually satisfied or satisfied again? And finally—be honest, aren't you tired of spending all your free time with women? I love my friends, but they can never fill the void only a man can fill. Male companionship is extremely important. If it were not true, God would never have created male and female to compliment one another.

   It has been a hard and oft times lonely road, but now that I am approaching middle age I can honestly say I'm okay. I have survived! And so will you if God chooses to keep you single. If you are young and single, please don't wait around for your 'knight in shining armor' to come sweep you off your feet, marry you, pay your bills, give you children and a house with a white picket fence. My friend, that may never happen. But then again it might. In the meantime, get busy with life. Do what you enjoy, pursue your gifts and use the talents God has given you. Get involved in your local church serving in a ministry you enjoy. Finally, enjoy your single life with friends and family.

   At nineteen, one year after giving my life to the Lord, I went to evangelism school. I then transferred to a four-year bible college where I took only courses of interest. I did not graduate—nor did I do well academically, but spiritually my roots in the faith started to grow deep in healthy soil. After a few years I attended nursing school where I did well academically and graduated. My nursing school degree led me to branch out into many different areas. I invested my extra money in some real estate and served the Lord on mission trips local and abroad. I also traveled for fun within the US and abroad. I fostered six babies (one at a time)as a ministry, and added three homes to my list of investments, all by the age of forty. God was blessing me abundantly. Now, years later, I wish I had enjoyed and appreciated His blessings a little more than I did. He truly will bless the single life if you let Him.

Also, wherever you go, make sure you take every opportunity to speak about your real groom—Jesus. He takes great pleasure when we share Him with others. Witnessing is one of the greatest joys in life. Whether single or married, we should all strive to share God's greatest gift; Salvation through faith in Jesus Christ.

Yes, it gets tiresome at times doing it alone. Obeying God is never easy. However, if God wants you single, then you must remain single. Are you ready to receive a "no" from God regarding marriage and children? Are you ready to be sold out for Christ—obeying Him? Are you ready to say "no" to not one man but to many because God sends you a red flag of warning?

For me, I have made peace with my single life. I never liked this life before, yet I realize my groom has always been right in front of me. I now know who my groom is——He is not someone who will be riding on a white horse to sweep me off my feet. Oh, my groom is coming for me, but He is coming for me in the clouds.

Finally, my sweet sisters in Christ, remember to delight in the Lord, regard Him as holy, and do not grumble. Understand God's protection and welcome it. Praise always and pray in the spirit asking God for His will for your life and not your own.

www.ingramcontent.com/pod-product-compliance
Lightning Source LLC
Chambersburg PA
CBHW072040060426
42449CB00010BA/2372